C000219576

gudetama™
surviving the holidays

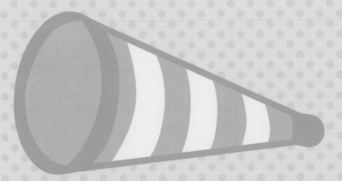

Sanrio®

written, illustrated, and lettered
by
wook-jin clark

Color flats by Jason Fischer

Edited by Sarah Gaydos and Robert Meyers.
Designed by Kate Z. Stone & Sonja Synak

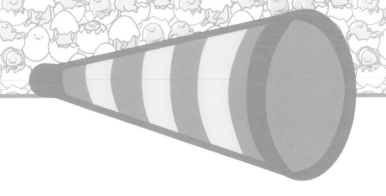

gudetama ™
surviving the holidays

ONI PRESS

Sanrio ®

Published by Oni-Lion Forge Publishing Group, LLC

James Lucas Jones, president & publisher • Sarah Gaydos, editor in chief • Charlie Chu, e.v.p. of creative & business development • Brad Rooks, director of operations • Amber O'Neill, special projects manager • Harris Fish, events manager • Margot Wood, director of marketing & sales • Devin Funches, sales & marketing manager • Katie Sainz, marketing manager • Tara Lehmann, publicist • Troy Look, director of design & production • Kate Z. Stone, senior graphic designer • Sonja Synak, graphic designer Hilary Thompson, graphic designer • Sarah Rockwell, junior graphic designer • Angie Knowles, digital prepress lead • Vincent Kukua, digital prepress technician • Jasmine Amiri, senior editor • Shawna Gore, senior editor • Amanda Meadows, senior editor • Robert Meyers, senior editor, licensing • Grace Bornhoft, editor • Zack Soto, editor • Chris Cerasi, editorial coordinator • Steve Ellis, vice president of games Ben Eisner, game developer • Michelle Nguyen, executive assistant • Jung Lee, logistics coordinator

Joe Nozemack, publisher emeritus

1319 SE Martin Luther King, Jr. Blvd. Suite 240
Portland, OR 97214

onipress.com   lionforge.com
onipress 🅕 🅞 🅖 lionforge

sanrio.com
🅕 gudetama
🅞 gudetamatweets
🅖 gudetama/

wookjinclark.com
🅞 wookjinclark

gudetama™
by Sanrio®

©2013, 2020 SANRIO CO., LTD.
Used Under License.
www.sanrio.com

SIL-34865

First Edition: October 2020
Retail ISBN 978-1-62010-819-2
Oni Exclusive Variant ISBN 978-1-62010-871-0
eISBN 978-1-62010-827-7
1 2 3 4 5 6 7 8 9 10
Library of Congress Control Number
2020937797
Printed in USA.
Retail Cover by Wook-Jin Clark
Oni Exclusive Variant Cover by Derek Charm

to be continued...

to be continued...

end.

wook jin clark

was born in South Korea and raised in South Carolina.
He loves coffee, doodling, walking around, and COFFEE!!
Look for his work in Image Comic's *Flavor*, Boom's *Bee
and Puppycat*, *Regular Show, Adventure Time*, and
Bravest Warriors comics.

making of gudetama ™
surviving the holidays
by Wook-Jin Clark

It all starts out with a script!

PAGE 1: *Introduction Page with Gudetama and Nisetama.*

Panel 1: *Nisteama is happily dancing in the snow, possibly ice skating. He's wearing an ugly Menorah sweater for Hanukkah. In the background we see a snowman, a Christmas tree, some Hanukkah decorations and some Kwanzaa decorations. Gudetama has a little Santa hat on.*

> **Gudetama:** Why are you making so much noise…?
> **Gudetama:** I just got comfortable.

Panel 2: *Nisteama is placing things on a snowman, while Gudetama is lying down amongst Christmas decorations.*

> **Nisetama:** Gudetama! This is my favorite time of the year!
> **Nisetama:** Aren't you excited?
> **Gudetama:** Don't make me do…things…

Panel 3: *CU of Nisetama leans into a lazy Gudetama and pleads.*

> **Nisetama:** But we have to! It's the holidays! It's such a busy time of year, and can be really difficult for some folks. People need our help, now more than ever!
> **Gudetama:** …fine.

Panel 4: *Nisetama is pulling back the page like in previous books, but this time the paper being pulled back looks like wrapping paper on the underside.*

> **Nisetama:** And away we go!

And then on to pencils!

Next, I ink the pages.

And finally, they are colored & lettered!

read more from oni press!

RICK AND MORTY™, VOL. 1

By Zac Gorman, CJ Cannon with Ryan Hill and Marc Ellerby

The hit comic book series based on Dan Harmon and Justin Roiland's hilarious [adult swim]™ animated show!

SCOTT PILGRIM COLOR COLLECTION, VOL. 1

By Bryan Lee O'Malley
with colors by Nathan Fairbairn

The *New York Times* bestselling series and basis for the movie *Scott Pilgrim vs. The World* is now available in a new softcover format!

THE TEA DRAGON SOCIETY

By Katie O'Neill

A multiple award-winning, gentle fantasy that follows the story of a blacksmith apprentice and the people she meets as she becomes entwined in the enchanting world of tea dragons.

KIM REAPER, VOL. 1: GRIM BEGINNINGS

By Sarah Graley

An adorable and hilarious supernatural rom-com.

la la la ~